WHAT'S NEXT ?

Volume 2

D1476111

A Pattern Discovery Approach
to
Problem Solving

Wilbert Reimer
Fresno Pacific College

Elaine Reimer, Editor

Reneé Mason, Illustrator
Roxanne Williams, Desktop Publisher

AIMS Education Foundation
Fresno, California

This book contains materials developed by the AIMS Education Foundation. **AIMS** (**A**ctivities **I**ntegrating **M**athematics and **S**cience) began in 1981 with a grant from the National Science Foundation. The non-profit AIMS Education Foundation publishes hands-on instructional materials (books and the monthly *AIMS* magazine) that integrate curricular disciplines such as mathematics, science, language arts, and social studies. The Foundation sponsors a national program of professional development through which educators may gain both an understanding of the AIMS philosophy and expertise in teaching by integrated, hands-on methods.

ISBN 1-881431-55-X

Printed in the United States of America

TABLE OF CONTENTS

INTRODUCTION

APPENDIX

SOLUTIONS

FIGURING OUT *WHAT'S NEXT ?*

Searching for patterns might well be the most important experience the student will have in mathematics.

Using patterns to make discoveries leads students to a greater understanding of both mathematics and the world. *What's Next?* implements a pattern discovery approach to problem solving. Difficult problems become simpler when order and relationships are uncovered. With such an approach, "students have opportunities to generalize and describe patterns and functions in many ways and to explore the relationships among them" (National Council of Teachers of Mathematics, 1989). This series should inspire students to learn, understand, and continually ask "What's next?"

Each volume of *What's Next?* contains life-related problems which address concepts from every area of mathematics. They are adaptable to a wide range of student abilities and may be explored in any sequence. Students gain valuable experience by seeing and identifying patterns. Teachers may want to begin with those activities that invite students to draw the next figure or guess the next number in a sequence. These will build pattern recognition confidence.

Many activities ask students to construct a table and continue a pattern. Once data are collected and recorded in a table, the pattern becomes easier to recognize. Students use the pattern they discover to complete the table and solve the problem. Often students are challenged to find a general formula for the problem. This step "builds readiness for a generalized view of mathematics" (National Council of Teachers of Mathematics, 1989).

Students should be familiar with the dominant patterns in mathematics such as those in square numbers, triangular numbers, and Pascal's Triangle. These and other helpful tools for understanding the role of patterns in problem solving are provided in the *Appendix* and the *Solutions*.

The Wishful Thinking Method

Dr. George Pólya, renowned author and teacher of problem solving, often advised, "If you have a difficult problem, wish for an easier one!" This "wish" is actually the first step of a powerful method for making discoveries. The wishful thinking method is encouraged throughout the activities in *What's Next?* Students are often asked to consider a simpler problem first. Using patterns makes the original problem surprisingly easy!

Vertical Solutions:

When working on a problem that uses a table, look for a vertical pattern in the second column. Examine the differences of the numbers in the second column. If this does not reveal a pattern, look at the differences of the differences, etc. This process works amazingly well. Remember, the *differences* are the key!

For many students, finding the vertical pattern in the second column will provide an appropriate challenge. The activities serve as excellent problem solving experiences without moving beyond this level.

Horizontal Solutions:

Students ready to advance to the next level of problem solving may examine the horizontal relationship between the numbers in the columns. They should ask, "What must be done to the number in the first column to obtain the number in the second column?" Once the horizontal relationship has been discovered, it may be expressed in mathematical language as a generalizing formula.

A sample problem will illustrate how the wishful thinking method works. More hints for finding patterns appear in the *Solutions*.

Sample Problem:

Find the sum of the first 50 even numbers.

$$2 + 4 + 6 + 8 + 10 + \ldots = ?$$

A first reaction to this problem might be: "I wish I had an easier problem!"

Simplify the problem and record your discoveries in a table.

Number of Terms	Sum
1	2
2	6
3	12
4	20
5	30
n	n(n+1)

Find the sums of series with one term, two terms, three terms, and so on. Continue adding and recording your results in the table.

Looking at a number of simpler cases is the first step of the wishful thinking problem solving approach.

 Vertical solution for sample problem:

Examine the numbers in the second column (2, 6, 12, 20, and 30). Notice that their differences are 4, 6, 8, and 10. A vertical pattern has been discovered! This discovery makes it possible to continue the vertical pattern in the second column indefinitely.

 Horizontal solution for sample problem:

The horizontal solution challenges the student to discover what must be done to the number in the first column to get the number in the second column. In this case, the student must multiply the number in the first column by a number one larger. In mathematical language, the horizontal solution would be written as n(n+1), where n represents any number in the first column.

What's Next for you?

Complete solutions to every activity are provided in the back of this book, along with suggestions and ideas for making the experience of pattern recognition valuable and practical. Don't be surprised if students discover patterns beyond the ones identified in the *Solutions*. One of the joys of mathematics—especially of problem solving—is that there is usually more than one way to solve a problem. Use these activities to stimulate and encourage student creativity. What's next? Hopefully, the satisfaction of understanding and the joy of discovery!

National Council of Teachers of Mathematics. *Curriculum and Evaluation Standards for School Mathematics.* Reston, VA.: NCTM, 1989.

WHAT'S MISSING ?

Patterns surround us every day, but sometimes we don't see them. Continue these sequences by predicting what's missing.

1. Two, four, six, eight, _____ , _____ , _____

2. One, three, two, four, three, _____ , _____

3. 3, 6, 9, _____ , _____ , _____

4. a, b, d, g, _____ , _____ , _____

5. 10, 8, 14, 12, 18, _____ , _____ , _____ , _____

6. z, x, v, _____ , _____ , _____ , _____

7. 1, 3, 6, 10, _____ , _____ , _____

8.  _____

9. 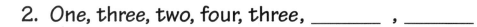 _____

10.  ___ ___ ___

11.  _____

12. _____

1

FOLLOW THE ORDERS !

These numbers in ordered pairs are related to each other. Discover what holds these pairs together and fill in the blanks.

1. (1, 2), (3, 4), (5, 6), (0, ___), (10, 11), (2, ___), (___ , 7), (8, ___)

2. (2, 4), (6, 12), (___ , 6), (4, ___), (13, ___), (___ , 10)

3. (9, 3), (3, 1), (12, ___), (___ , 2), (15, ___), (___ , 8)

4. (1, 3), (7, 9), (3, 5), (8, ___), (16, ___), (___ , 13), (6, ___)

5. (4, 0), (2, 0), (9, 0), (12, ___), (6, ___), (22, ___)

6. (4, 16), (7, 49), (5, ___), (___ , 64), (10, ___), (___ , 36)

7. (4, 9), (5, 11), (2, 5), (6, ___), (___ , 7), (10, ___), (___ , 3)

8. (10, 2), (25, 5), (5, 1), (35, ___), (50, ___), (___ , 9), (___ , 3)

9. (24, 3), (16, 2), (40, 5), (32, ___), (___ , 7), (64, ___)

10. (3, 10), (6, 37), (2, 5), (7, ___), (5, ___), (___ , 2), (___ , 82)

11. (88, 8), (44, 4), (55, ___), (11, ___), (___ , 6), (___ , 10)

12. (12, 8), (6, 5), (10, 7), (14, ___), (20, ___), (___ , 14), (100, ___)

EXTRA CHALLENGES:

1. (3, 6), (8, 56), (5, 20), (6, ___), (10, ___), (4, ___)

2. (16, 2), (64, 4), (36, 3), (100, ___), (4, ___), (144, ___)

NAME THAT NUMBER !

Complete the following tables.

1	5
2	7
3	9
4	11
5	
6	
50	
n	

1	3
2	6
3	11
4	18
5	
6	
50	
n	

1	7
2	10
3	13
4	16
5	
6	
50	
n	

1	8
2	13
3	18
4	23
5	
6	
50	
n	

1	1
2	5
3	9
4	13
5	
6	
50	
n	

1	0
2	3
3	8
4	15
5	
6	
50	
n	

Make up some tables of your own.

FIGURE IT OUT

If these patterns are continued, how many dots will be in the 100th figure of each sequence?

1. Fig.1   Fig.2   Fig.3

2. Fig.1   Fig.2   Fig.3

3. Fig.1   Fig.2   Fig.3

4. Fig.1   Fig.2   Fig.3

5. Fig.1   Fig.2   Fig.3

Make up some of your own figures!

EASY AS PIE !

How many pieces will result from 10 cuts through the center of a pie?

To solve this problem, first examine a pie with one cut, then pies with two and three cuts. Continue until you see the pattern.

1 cut   2 cuts   3 cuts

Use the chart to record your results.

Number of Cuts	Number of Pieces
1	2
2	4
3	
4	
5	
6	
7	
8	
9	
10	
20	
n	

A BANQUET AT TONY'S

Tony's Restaurant has eight small tables that will be used for a banquet. Each table seats only one person on a side. If the tables are pushed together to make one long table, how many people can be seated?

To solve this problem, first look at an easier problem. Count how many people can sit around one table. How many can sit around two tables?

Use the pattern you discover to solve the problem.

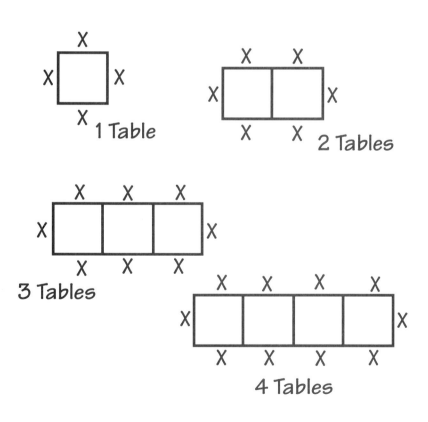

1 Table

2 Tables

3 Tables

4 Tables

Number of Tables	Number of People
1	4
2	6
3	
4	
5	
6	
7	
8	
30	
n	

THREE FOR ME

Discover the patterns in the triples and fill in the missing numbers.

Triple Pattern #1

(1, 3, 6)
(4, 12, 24)
(5, 15, 30)
(10, ___ , ___)
(___ , 18, ___)
(___ , ___ , 42)

Triple Pattern #2

(1, 3, 6)
(5, 7, 10)
(19, 21, 24)
(8, 10, 13)
(31, 33, 36)
(___ , 17, ___)
(45, ___ , ___)
(___ , 51, ___)
(___ , ___ , 93)

Triple Pattern #3

(1, 5, 10)
(2, 6, 12)
(8, 12, 24)
(6, ___ , ___)
(14, ___ , ___)
(___ , ___ , 30)
(___ , 16, ___)
(___ , 60, ___)

Triple Pattern #4

(6, 36, 12)
(5, 30, 10)
(2, 12, 4)
(4, 24, 8)
(3, ___ , 6)
(___ , 60 , ___)
(7, ___ , ___)
(11, ___ , ___)

Triple Pattern #5

(2, 3, 10)
(3, 5, 16)
(4, 6, 20)
(6, 1, 14)
(5, 8, ___)
(1, 7, ___)
(8, ___ , 30)
(10, ___ , 48)
(___ , 12, 40)

Make up some of your own triples. Remember that all triples must be connected together by patterns.

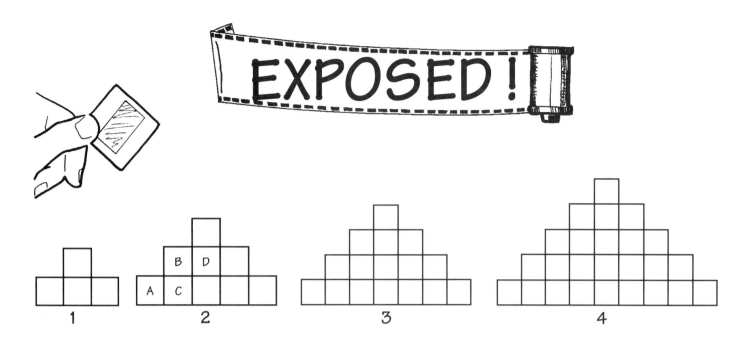

Square A is exposed on three sides, B on two sides, C on one side, and D on no sides. Examine the figures and complete the table.

Find a pattern and predict the results for the 5th and nth figures.

Figure	Height in Squares	Number of Squares	Squares Exposed On			
			No Sides	1 Side	2 Sides	3 Sides
1	2	4	0	1	0	3
2	3					
3						
4						
5						
n						

ODD DENOMINATORS

$$\frac{1}{1 \cdot 3} + \frac{1}{3 \cdot 5} + \frac{1}{5 \cdot 7} + \frac{1}{7 \cdot 9} + \frac{1}{9 \cdot 11} + \cdots$$

What is the sum of the first 50 terms in this series?

Finding the sum of a series often becomes easier by looking at simpler cases. Instead of trying to add all 50 terms, add the first term, then the first two, the first three, and so on. Continue until you find a pattern.

This pattern will help you solve the problem!
Use the table to record your results.

Number of Terms	Sum
1	$\frac{1}{3}$
2	
3	
4	
5	
6	
7	
50	

EXTRA CHALLENGE:

What is the sum of the first n terms?

FROM FRACTIONS TO DECIMALS

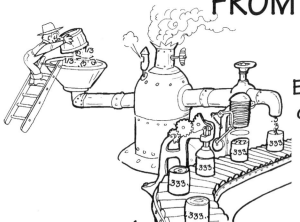

Every rational number (a fraction made of two integers) becomes a decimal with a pattern when the denominator is divided into the numerator.

For example, $\dfrac{1}{11}$ = .09090909....   and $\dfrac{1}{7}$ = .142857142857142857...

Write the first twenty decimal places for each fraction. As soon as you see the pattern, use it to predict the remaining digits.

a. $\dfrac{4}{9}$ = . _

b. $\dfrac{1}{33}$ = . _

c. $\dfrac{1}{13}$ = . _

d. $\dfrac{1}{37}$ = . _

e. $\dfrac{1}{27}$ = . _

f. $\dfrac{1}{41}$ = . _

g. $\dfrac{21}{111}$ = . _

h. $\dfrac{100}{333}$ = . _

CRISS-CROSSED SUMS

Find three more crosses in this multiplication chart. Compare the center number with the sum of the five numbers in each cross. Record the information you discover in the table.

x	0	1	2	3	4	5	6	7	8	9
0	0	0	0	0	0	0	0	0	0	0
1	0	1	2	3	4	5	6	7	8	9
2	0	2	4	6	8	10	12	14	16	18
3	0	3	6	9	12	15	18	21	24	27
4	0	4	8	12	16	20	24	28	32	36
5	0	5	10	15	20	25	30	35	40	45
6	0	6	12	18	24	30	36	42	48	54
7	0	7	14	21	28	35	42	49	56	63
8	0	8	16	24	32	40	48	56	64	72
9	0	9	18	27	36	45	54	63	72	81

Center Number	Sum of the Five Numbers
8	40
12	60
n	

Cross 1: 6 / 4 8 12 / 10

Cross 2: 6 / 10 12 14 / 18

What pattern do you discover?

UP AND COMING TRIANGLES

How many triangles are pointing up in this equilateral triangle?

Solve this problem by first looking at some easier problems. Begin with an equilateral triangle with sides measuring one unit, then two units, three units, etc. Do you see a pattern?

Use your discovery to solve the original problem!

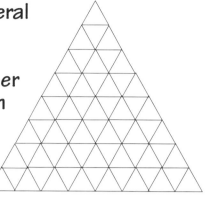

Side Measurement	Number of Triangles Pointing Up
1	1
2	4
3	
4	
5	
6	
7	
8	

EXTRA CHALLENGE:

Solve this problem for an equilateral triangle with sides measuring n units each.

12

SIDE BY SIDE

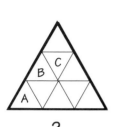

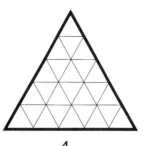
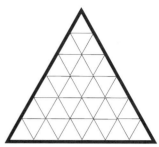

1   2   3   4   5

Triangle A is exposed on two sides, B on one side, and C on no sides.

Use the diagrams to complete the table. Find a pattern and predict the results for the 6th and nth figures.

Triangle	Length of Side	Number of Triangles	Number of Triangles Exposed On		
			No Sides	1 Side	2 Sides
1	2	4	1	0	3
2	3				
3	4				
4					
5					
6					
n					

WHAT'S YOUR ANGLE ?

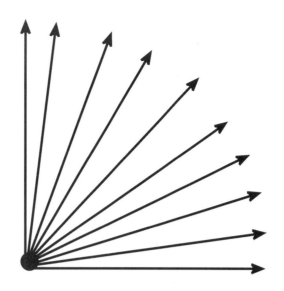

How many angles do you see?

Number of Rays	Total Number of Angles
2	1
3	3
4	
5	
6	
7	
8	
9	
10	

Use the diagrams to complete the table. Find a pattern in your answers that will help you solve the problem.

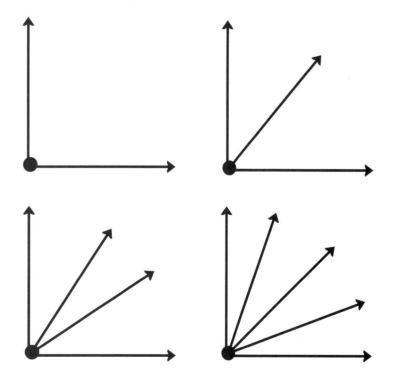

EXTRA CHALLENGE:

How many angles are there with n rays?

NUMBER 999 IS A FRIEND OF MINE

Find the products below and watch for a pattern in your answers. As soon as you discover the pattern, use it to make multiplying by 999 easy!

Find these products.

999 • 121 = 120,879

999 • 237 = __ __ __ , __ __ __

999 • 312 = __ __ __ , __ __ __

999 • 369 = __ __ __ , __ __ __

999 • 426 = __ __ __ , __ __ __

999 • 576 = __ __ __ , __ __ __

999 • 643 = __ __ __ , __ __ __

999 • 790 = __ __ __ , __ __ __

Describe the pattern you have discovered.

999 • 834 = __ __ __ , __ __ __

999 • 900 = __ __ __ , __ __ __

Predict these products without multiplying.

999 • 146 = __ __ __ , __ __ __   999 • 674 = __ __ __ , __ __ __

999 • 257 = __ __ __ , __ __ __   999 • 712 = __ __ __ , __ __ __

999 • 343 = __ __ __ , __ __ __   999 • 999 = __ __ __ , __ __ __

999 • 445 = __ __ __ , __ __ __   Multiply to check your answers!

ARRAYS THAT AMAZE !

Arrays hold mysterious patterns just waiting to be found! Study this array carefully. Find at least three patterns.

```
                1

            2   3   4

        5   6   7   8   9

    10  11  12  13  14  15  16

17  18  19  20  21  22  23  24  25
```

What number appears in the middle of the 50th row? the nth row?

Complete the table to help you.

Row Number	Middle Number
1	1
2	3
3	
4	
5	
50	
n	

EXTRA CHALLENGE:

Use a pattern found in the array to determine which number would be directly below 400.

WHAT'S HAPPENIN' ?

When a coin is tossed, it may land "heads" or "tails." A sample space (which lists all possible outcomes) for tossing a penny and a nickel would look like this:

Penny	Nickel
H	H
H	T
T	H
T	T

Study the sample spaces for tossing one coin, two coins, and three coins. Look carefully at the vertical patterns in each column. Use these patterns to construct sample spaces for tossing four coins and five coins.

5 COINS

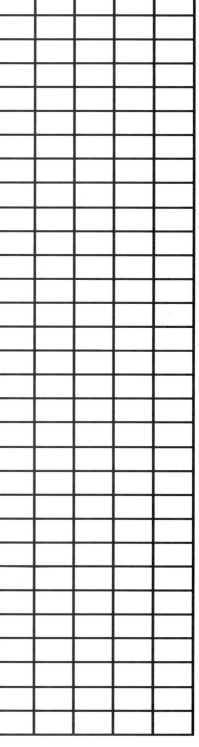

1 COIN

H
T

2 COINS

H	H
H	T
T	H
T	T

3 COINS

H	H	H
H	H	T
H	T	H
H	T	T
T	H	H
T	H	T
T	T	H
T	T	T

4 COINS

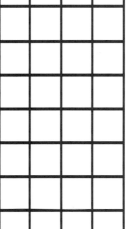

FLIP FOR IT !

If six coins are tossed, what is the probability that exactly three will show heads? Most people guess 50 percent. Is this right?

Look at the patterns that emerge when tossing coins. Use your sample spaces from the *What's Happenin'?* activity to help you complete the table.

Number of Coins	Probability of Tossing Exactly						
	0 Heads	1 Head	2 Heads	3 Heads	4 Heads	5 Heads	6 Heads
1							
2							
3							
4							
5							
6							

Use the pattern you discover to predict the results when six coins are tossed. Does the pattern resemble any others you've studied?

Hint: Look at Pascal's triangle.

TOSS FOR TRIANGLES

What is the probability that a triangle can be constructed from three line segments whose lengths are determined by tossing three dice?

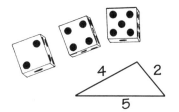 MAKE A GUESS: _____ %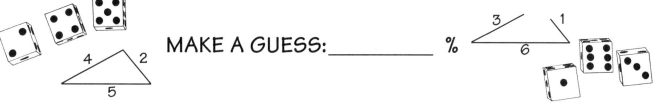

To solve this problem, make a list of all possible outcomes. This list, called a sample space, is begun for you here, but you will need a separate sheet of paper because there are 216 possibilities!

Use an orderly process to record the possibilities, and note which outcomes would create triangles.

Remember, a triangle is possible only if the two shorter sides add up to more than the longest side.

Sample Space			
1	1	1	triangle
1	1	2	no triangle
1	1	3	no triangle
1	1	4	no triangle
1	1	5	no triangle
1	1	6	no triangle
1	2	1	no triangle
1	2	2	triangle
1	2	3	no triangle
1	2	4	no triangle
1	2	5	no triangle
1	2	6	no triangle
1	3	1	no triangle
		Etc.	

PROBABILITY OF TRIANGLE: _____ %

How does your guess compare with your discovery?

EXTRA CHALLENGE:

Toss three dice 100 times and keep track of how many triangles you can create. How does your experimental result compare with the solution you found?

BLOCK BLITZ

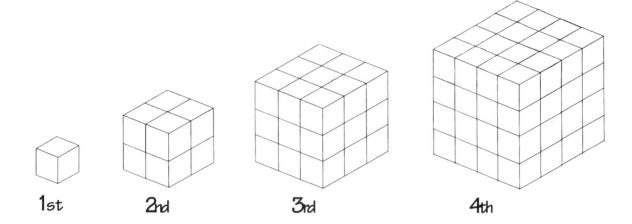

1st   2nd   3rd   4th

Suppose you would like to continue building block structures like the ones above. What is the <u>total</u> number of blocks you would need to build eight structures?

To solve this problem, count the total number of blocks needed for the first structure, then the first two, etc.

Complete the chart. Try to discover a pattern!

Number of Structures	Total Number of Blocks
1	1
2	9
3	
4	
5	
6	
7	
8	

EXTRA CHALLENGE:

Without continuing the chart, determine how many blocks are needed to construct 20 structures. How many blocks are needed for n structures?

ROWING WITH PASCAL

What is the sum of the numbers in the 10th row of Pascal's triangle? Devise an easy way to discover the answer. Add the numbers in the first row, the second row, the third, and so on, until you see a pattern. Use the pattern to predict the answer.

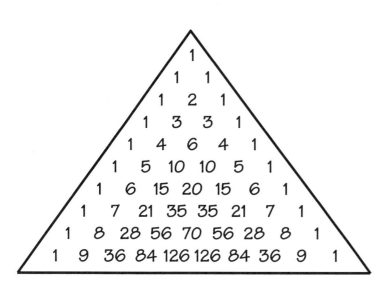

Pascal's Triangle

Row Number	Sum
1	1
2	2
3	4
4	
5	
6	
7	
8	
9	
10	

EXTRA CHALLENGE:

What is the sum of the numbers in the nth row?

ABOVE AVERAGE

Find the average of the first 50 terms of each sequence by completing the tables and discovering the patterns.

Example: 2, 4, 6, 8, 10, 12, ...

Number of Terms	Average
2	3
3	4
4	5
5	6
6	7
50	51

Average of first two terms:
$$\frac{2 + 4}{2} = 3$$

Average of first three terms:
$$\frac{2 + 4 + 6}{3} = 4$$

A. 1, 3, 5, 7, 9, 11, . . .

Number of Terms	Average
2	
3	
4	
5	
6	
50	

B. 6, 8, 10, 12, 14, . . .

Number of Terms	Average
2	
3	
4	
5	
6	
50	

C. 1, 2, 3, 4, 5, 6, . . .

Number of Terms	Average
2	
3	
4	
5	
6	
50	

D. 4, 8, 12, 16, 20, 24, . . .

Number of Terms	Average
2	
3	
4	
5	
6	
50	

MAGIC SQUARES

 A magic square is a square array of numbers in which the row, column, and diagonal sums are all equal. Place the first nine counting numbers (1, 2, 3, 4, 5, 6, 7, 8, 9) in the nine squares on the tortoise so that each row, column, and diagonal has a sum of 15.

Magic squares originated in China, as early as 2200 B.C. Tradition says that the first magic square appeared on the shell of a divine tortoise. We know there is nothing "magical" about these arrays, except perhaps their capacity to intrigue students of all times.

MAKING MAGIC SQUARES

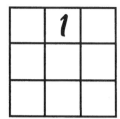

Construct an odd by odd magic square.

1. Place the 1st number in the middle square of the top row.

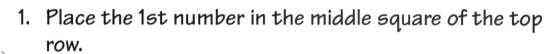

2. Place the 2nd number in the square located one square to the right and one square up. If such a move takes you off the grid, come back on at the bottom or on the left.

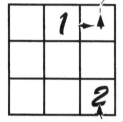

3. Repeat the sequence outlined in Step 2 until all squares are full. If a particular square is already filled, place the next number directly under the last number entered.

8	1	6
3	5	7
4	9	2

4. The last square filled should be in the middle of the bottom row. If your number sequence does not end in this way, the square has not been completed correctly.

Complete this 7 by 7 magic square using the first 49 counting numbers.

Complete this 5 by 5 magic square using the first 25 counting numbers.

MAGIC SQUARE MADNESS

When constructing magic squares, it is possible to vary the values of the first number (F), the increase (I) between entries, and the dimension (D) of the square. Once the choice is made for these values, the magic square is determined. Several magic squares with different values for F, I, and D are shown below.

15	1	11
5	9	13
7	17	3

F=1, I=2, D=3

34	6	26
14	22	30
18	38	10

F=6, I=4, D=3

49	70	1	22	43
67	13	19	40	46
10	16	37	58	64
28	34	55	61	7
31	52	73	4	25

F=1, I=3, D=5

Complete the magic squares using the given values for F, I, and D. Use the "one to the right, one up" method. Be sure to check the sums of all rows, columns, and diagonals to see if they are equal.

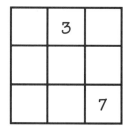

F=3, I=4, D=3

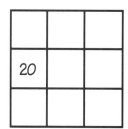

F=5, I=2, D=3

F=10, I=5, D=3

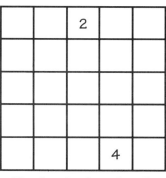

F=2, I=2, D=5

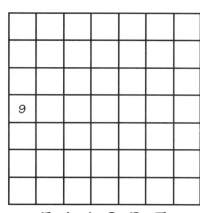

F=1, I=2, D=7

MAGIC SQUARE DISCOVERIES

There are six important values associated with every odd by odd magic square. These values are represented by letters and are explained in the key.

Inspect the magic squares below. Then, discover the <u>formulas</u> for:

     M, in terms of F and L.

     S, in terms of M and D.

     L, in terms of F, I, and D.

     S, in terms of F, I, and D.

16	2	12
6	10	14
8	18	4

F=2
I=2
L=18
M=10
D=3
S=30

25	4	19
10	16	22
13	28	7

F=4
I=3
L=28
M=16
D=3
S=48

92	119	146	5	32	59	86
116	143	23	29	56	83	89
140	20	26	53	80	107	113
17	44	50	77	104	110	137
41	47	74	101	128	134	14
65	71	98	125	131	11	38
68	95	122	149	8	35	62

F=5
I=3
L=149
M=77
D=7
S=539

33	47	1	15	29
45	9	13	27	31
7	11	25	39	43
19	23	37	41	5
21	35	49	3	17

F=1
I=2
L=49
M=25
D=5
S=125

A MAGIC COMPOSITION

A composite magic square is a large magic square made up of smaller magic squares. Study the 9 by 9 composite magic square. Find the pattern within the square and fill the remaining empty squares.

When completed, the large 9 by 9 grid will be a magic square. Each of the nine smaller 3 by 3 grids will also be a magic square!

			8	1	6			
			3	5	7			
			4	9	2			
	19							
						17	10	15
						12	14	16
						13	18	11

THE ACE CASE

There are six cards on a table. The cards are face down, but your friend has told you that two of the cards are aces. If you choose two cards, which is more likely?

(a) that you will pick one or both of the aces

OR

(b) that you will pick no aces

Suppose you label the cards one through six. Make a list of all possible two card combinations. You can do this by completing the sample space below.

Watch for patterns to help you construct your sample space.
Hint: There will be a total of 15 rows.

Sample Space:
1 and 2
1 and 3
1 and 4
1 and 5
1 and 6
2 and 3
2 and 4

_____
_____
_____
_____
_____
_____
_____
_____

Now, choose any two numbers to represent the aces. Count how many combinations include at least one "ace." Use these results to determine the following probabilities.

Probability of picking at least one ace = _____
Probability of picking no aces = _____

RINGS OF CIRCLES

Look what happens when circular objects (such as pennies or plastic chips) are arranged in rings around a central circle.

Count the circles in the designs with three and four rings and enter your results in the table. How many circles would be needed to create a design with eight rings? Discover the pattern in the second column and complete the table.

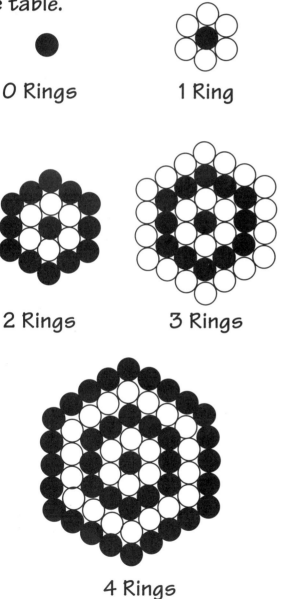

● **0 Rings**

1 Ring

2 Rings   **3 Rings**

4 Rings

Number of Rings	Total Number of Circles
0	1
1	7
2	19
3	
4	
5	
6	
7	
8	

EXTRA CHALLENGE:

How many circles would be needed for a design with n rings?

PATH PATTERNS

Suppose a craftsman has ten 1 by 2 tiles with which to cover a 2 by 10 rectangular path. In how many different ways can these ten tiles be arranged?

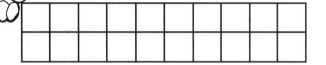

Solve this problem by first arranging tiles on a 2 by 1 rectangle, then a 2 by 2, and so on, until you discover the pattern that emerges. Record your results in the table.

2 by 1

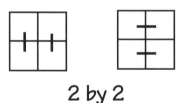

2 by 2

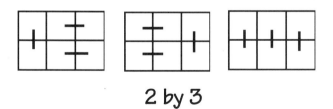

2 by 3

Dimensions	Number of Arrangements
2 by 1	1
2 by 2	2
2 by 3	3
2 by 4	_____ (not 4)
2 by 5	_____
2 by 6	_____
2 by 7	_____
2 by 8	_____
2 by 9	_____
2 by 10	_____

What famous number sequence does the pattern in the table resemble?

FIFTY TERM SUM - UP

4 + 8 + 12 + 16 + ...

What is the sum of the first 50 terms in this series?

Solve this problem by beginning with an easier one. Find the sum of a series with one term.   Next find the sum of the first two terms, the first three, etc. Look for the pattern that appears!

Record your results in the table. Use the pattern you discover to complete the table.

$$4 = 4$$
$$4 + 8 = 12$$
$$4 + 8 + 12 = ?$$
$$4 + 8 + 12 + 16 = ?$$

Number of Terms	Sum
1	4
2	12
3	
4	
5	
6	
7	
50	

EXTRA CHALLENGE:

Can you discover a general rule to find the sum of the first n terms in the series?

PRODUCT PATTERNS

When numbers are multiplied, patterns often emerge in their products. These patterns help to predict products and simplify the multiplication process. In this activity, explore what happens when numbers ending in five are squared.

Discover the pattern by examining the products in these examples.

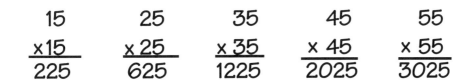

15	25	35	45	55
x15	x 25	x 35	x 45	x 55
225	625	1225	2025	3025

What do you observe about the last two digits in each product?

Now examine all but the last two digits in each product. What do you see?

Use what you have discovered to predict the products for the following.

65	75	85	95	105
x 65	x 75	x 85	x 95	x 105

THE HARMONIC TRIANGLE

This triangle is full of patterns just waiting to be discovered! Look for clues that will help you understand how it is constructed. Use your pattern recognition skills to complete the next three rows of the "harmonic triangle."

$$\frac{1}{1}$$

$$\frac{1}{2} \qquad \frac{1}{2}$$

$$\frac{1}{3} \qquad \frac{1}{6} \qquad \frac{1}{3}$$

$$\frac{1}{4} \qquad \frac{1}{12} \qquad \frac{1}{12} \qquad \frac{1}{4}$$

$$\frac{1}{5} \qquad \frac{1}{20} \qquad \frac{1}{30} \qquad \frac{1}{20} \qquad \frac{1}{5}$$

$$\frac{1}{6} \qquad \frac{1}{30} \qquad \frac{1}{60} \qquad \frac{1}{60} \qquad \frac{1}{30} \qquad \frac{1}{6}$$

—   —   —   —   —   —   —

—   —   —   —   —   —

—   —   —   —   —

HINT: Pascal's triangle and the harmonic triangle have some pattern similarities!

Describe some of the patterns you see in the triangle.

DO YOU HAVE CHANGE ?

How many ways can you make change for a quarter using any combination of pennies, nickels, and dimes?

Study the solution below. Do you see any patterns?

Dimes	Nickels	Pennies
2	1	0
2	0	5
1	3	0
1	2	5
1	1	10
1	0	15
0	5	0
0	4	5
0	3	10
0	2	15
0	1	20
0	0	25

There are 12 ways to make change for a quarter.

Use what you have observed to discover how many ways you can make change for a half-dollar using any combination of pennies, nickels, dimes, and quarters.

EXTRA CHALLENGE:

How many ways can you make change for a dollar using pennies, nickels, dimes, quarters, and half-dollars?

FIGURATE FAMILIES

Numbers that can be represented by dots arranged in specific geometric shapes are called figurate numbers. These numbers can be divided into "families" according to their shapes.

Complete the table below. Note the many horizontal and vertical relationships. Take advantage of these patterns as you work.

Rank of Family Members

Family	1st	2nd	3rd	4th	5th	6th	7th	8th
Triangular	1	3	6	10				
Square	1	4	9					
Pentagonal	1	5	12					
Hexagonal	1	6						
Heptagonal	1							
Octagonal								

PENTAGONAL NUMBERS

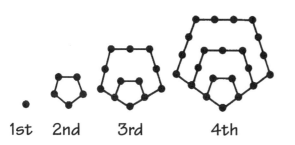

1st   2nd   3rd   4th

HEXAGONAL NUMBERS

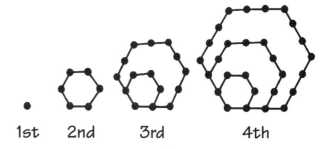

1st   2nd   3rd   4th

THE FLIP SIDE

$$\frac{1}{1} + \frac{1}{3} + \frac{1}{6} + \frac{1}{10} + \frac{1}{15} + \frac{1}{21} + \frac{1}{28} + \frac{1}{36} + \cdots$$

Discover the pattern in the sums of "flipped" or inverted triangular numbers and complete the table. Express each sum as a common fraction.

QUESTIONS:

1. When the number in the left column is odd, how does one find the numerator of the sum? the denominator?

2. When the number in the left column is even, how does one find the numerator of the sum? the denominator?

3. Without continuing the table, predict the sum of the first
   (a) 80 inverted triangular numbers.
   (b) 127 inverted triangular numbers.
   (c) 1000 inverted triangular numbers.

4. What does the sum approach as more terms are added?

Number of Inverted Triangular Numbers	Sum
1	$\frac{1}{1}$
2	$\frac{4}{3}$
3	$\frac{3}{2}$
4	$\frac{8}{5}$
5	
6	
7	
8	
9	
10	

WHITE-FACED CUBES

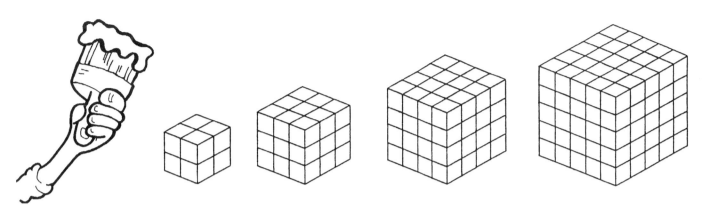

Suppose wooden cubes of various sizes are painted white and cut into smaller cubes as shown above.

How many smaller cubes have three white faces? two white faces? one white face? no white faces?

Complete the table and discover the many patterns that emerge.

Length of Edge	Number of Cubes Formed	Number with 3 White Faces	Number with 2 White Faces	Number with 1 White Face	Number with No White Faces
2					
3					
4					
5					
6					
20					
n					

CHECKERBOARD CHALLENGE

How many squares are there on an 8 by 8 checkerboard? Did you guess 64? Think again! How many squares of *all sizes* are there?

To solve this problem, count the squares on several smaller boards and record the numbers in the table.

Don't count squares on the larger boards! When you see the pattern, use it as a shortcut to complete the table.

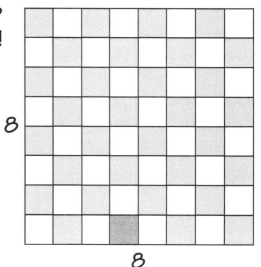

8

8

1 by 1

2 by 2

3 by 3

Dimension of Board	Number of Squares
1 by 1	1
2 by 2	5
3 by 3	
4 by 4	
5 by 5	
6 by 6	
7 by 7	
8 by 8	

A MATTER OF DEGREES

The sum of the angles in any triangle is always equal to 180 degrees. These angles can be arranged to show that they equal 180 degrees.

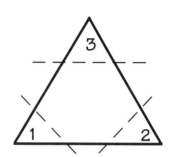

To find the sum of the angles in any polygon, subdivide it into triangles by drawing all possible diagonals from one vertex.

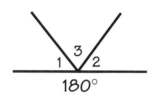

180°

Complete the table to discover a formula which gives the sum of the angles for any polygon with n sides.

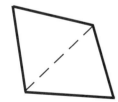

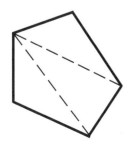

Number of Sides	Number of Diagonals from One Vertex	Number of Triangles Made	Sum of Interior Angles
3	0	1	180°
4	1	2	
5			
6			
7			
8			
n			

39

THE SNOWFLAKE CURVE

Would you believe that a geometric figure with area less than one square inch can have a perimeter of more than 100 million miles?

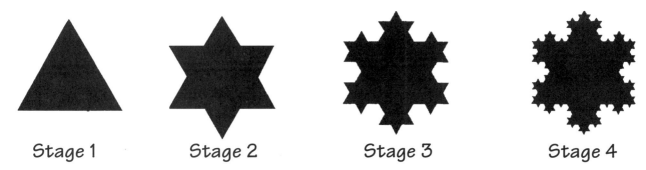

| Stage 1 | Stage 2 | Stage 3 | Stage 4 |

Each side of the equilateral triangle in Stage 1 is divided into thirds. Smaller equilateral triangles are placed on the middle third of each side in Stage 2. When this process is repeated, the curve begins to resemble a snowflake!

Discover the patterns and complete the table. Assume each side of the original equilateral triangle measures one inch.

Stage Number	Number of Sides	Length of Each Side (in inches)
1	3	1
2	12	$\frac{1}{3}$
3	48	$\frac{1}{9}$
4	192	$\frac{1}{27}$
5		
n		

Write a formula for finding the perimeter of the nth stage.

With a scientific calculator, find the perimeter (in miles) of the snowflake in the (a) 60th stage and (b) 100th stage.

REPEATING RECTANGLES

If the figures shown were cut along all lines, how many rectangles would result from Figure 50? Complete the table and discover the pattern to solve this problem.

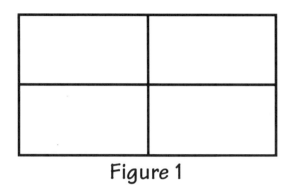

Figure 1

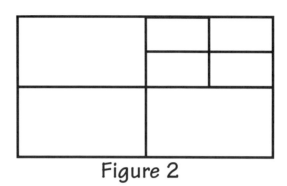

Figure 2

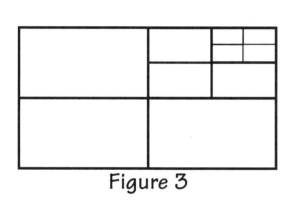

Figure 3

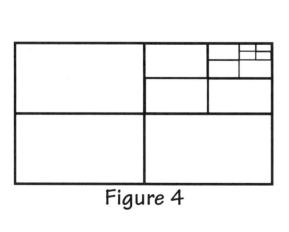

Figure 4

Figure	Number of Rectangles
1	4
2	7
3	
4	
5	
6	
7	
50	
n	

KNIGHT PAIRS ON THE CHESSBOARD

In the game of chess, a knight moves two squares in any direction, then one more square at a right angle. On an 8 by 8 chessboard we can find many pairs of squares (knight pairs) which are a knight's move apart. For example, on the board shown, squares A and B are a knight's move apart. Two other such pairs are squares B and E and squares C and D.

How many knight pairs are there on an

    (a) 8 by 8 chessboard?
    (b) n by n chessboard?

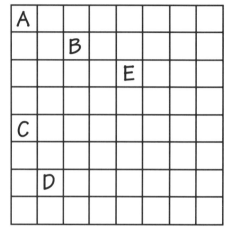

Solve this problem by first examining some easier cases. Determine how many knight pairs exist on 3 by 3, 4 by 4, and 5 by 5 boards. The squares are lettered to help you list and count the pairs. Use the pattern that emerges to solve the original problem.

Size of Board	Number of Knight Pairs
3 by 3	
4 by 4	
5 by 5	
6 by 6	
7 by 7	
8 by 8	
n by n	

A	B	C
D	E	F
G	H	I

3 by 3 Board

A	B	C	J
D	E	F	K
G	H	I	L
P	O	N	M

4 by 4 Board

A	B	C	J	Q
D	E	F	K	R
G	H	I	L	S
P	O	N	M	T
Z	Y	X	V	U

5 by 5 Board

DIAGONAL CHALLENGE

Predict how many diagonals can be drawn in polygons with eight, nine, and ten sides.

Count the diagonals as you draw them for the six and seven-sided polygons. Record the number of diagonals in the table. When all possible diagonals have been drawn, the number drawn from each vertex should be the same.

Without drawing polygons, use the pattern in the table to predict the answers for eight, nine, and ten-sided polygons.

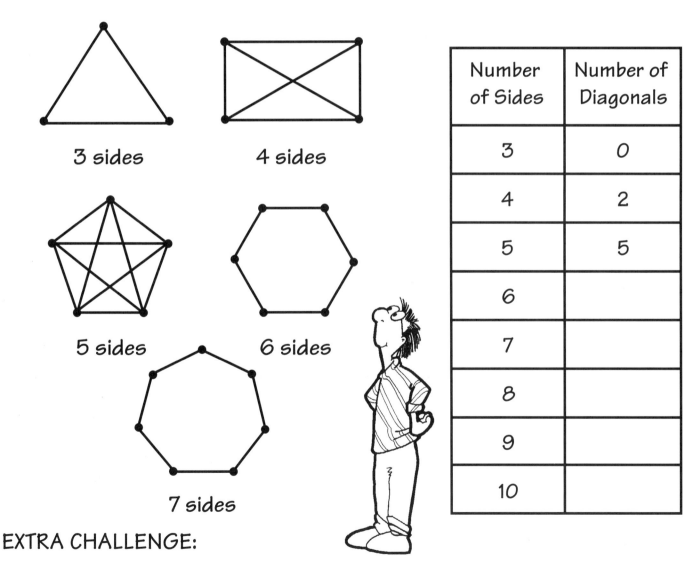

3 sides	4 sides
5 sides	6 sides
7 sides	

Number of Sides	Number of Diagonals
3	0
4	2
5	5
6	
7	
8	
9	
10	

EXTRA CHALLENGE:

State a formula for finding the number of diagonals in a polygon with n sides.

REGION REVENGE

If 10 points were placed on a circle so that the segments connecting points created the maximum number of regions, how many regions would be created?

Count the regions in a circle with one point, two points, three points, and so on, until you see the pattern. Predict how many regions would be created in circles with eight, nine, and ten points without actually drawing them.

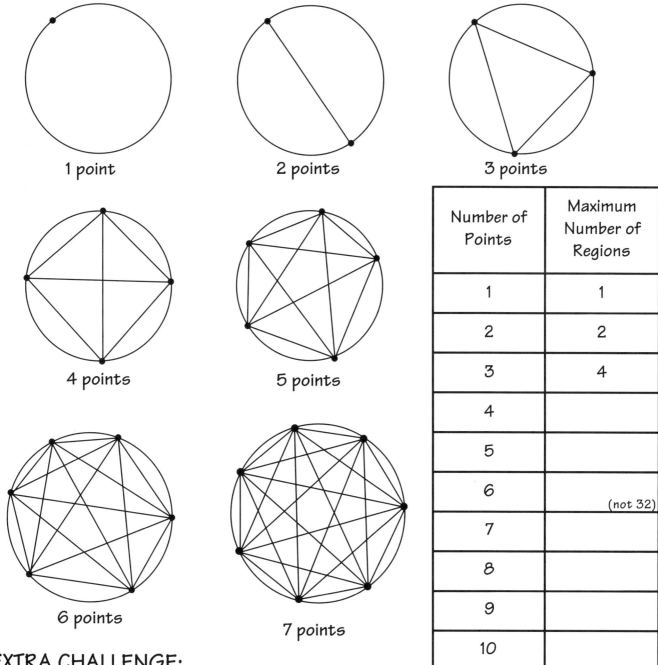

1 point

2 points

3 points

4 points

5 points

6 points

7 points

Number of Points	Maximum Number of Regions
1	1
2	2
3	4
4	
5	
6	(not 32)
7	
8	
9	
10	

EXTRA CHALLENGE:
Determine the number of regions in a circle with n points.

APPENDIX

PASCAL'S TRIANGLE

THE SOURCE OF MANY PATTERNS

```
                        1
                      1   1
                    1   2   1
                  1   3   3   1
                1   4   6   4   1
              1   5  10  10   5   1
            1   6  15  20  15   6   1
          1   7  21  35  35  21   7   1
        1   8  28  56  70  56  28   8   1
      1   9  36  84 126 126  84  36   9   1
    1  10  45 120 210 252 210 120  45  10   1
  1  11  55 165 330 462 462 330 165  55  11   1
```

SQUARE, OBLONG, AND TRIANGULAR NUMBERS

Square numbers are numbers which can be represented by dots in a square array. The first four square numbers are pictured below.

1st 2nd 3rd 4th

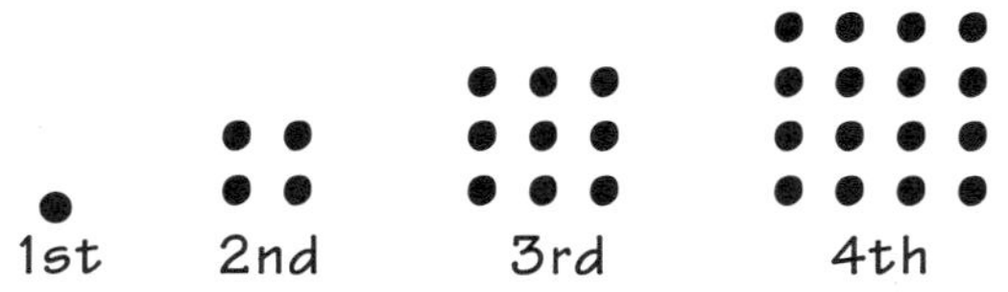

Square Number	Number of Dots
1st	1
2nd	4
3rd	9
4th	16
5th	25
6th	36
50th	2500
nth	n^2

Oblong numbers are numbers which can be represented by dots in a rectangle having one dimension one unit longer than the other. The first four oblong numbers are pictured below.

1st 2nd 3rd 4th

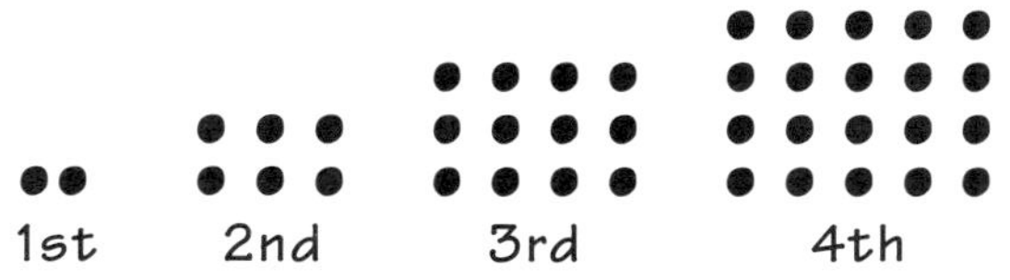

Oblong Number	Number of Dots
1st	2
2nd	6
3rd	12
4th	20
5th	30
6th	42
50th	2550
nth	$n(n+1)$

Triangular numbers are numbers which can be represented by dots in a triangular array. The first four triangular numbers are pictured below.

1st 2nd 3rd 4th

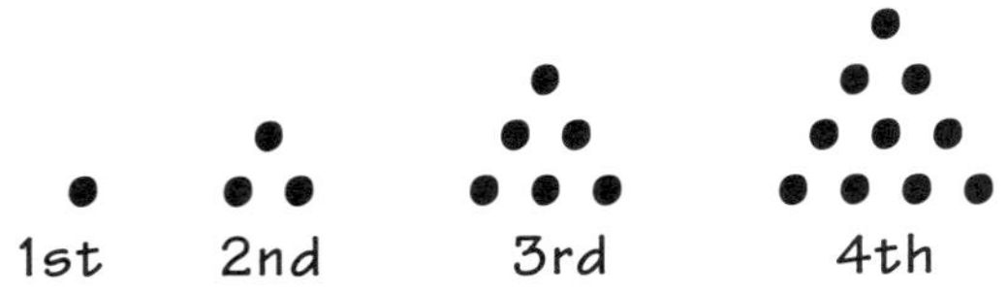

Triangular Number	Number of Dots
1st	1
2nd	3
3rd	6
4th	10
5th	15
6th	21
50th	1275
nth	$\frac{n(n+1)}{2}$

THE METHOD OF FINITE DIFFERENCES

For some of the extra challenges in *What's Next?* the horizontal solutions are fairly complex. An effective approach to these problems is the method of finite differences. This method may be applied to find a horizontal solution (general formula) whenever a *constant* difference occurs between numbers in a sequence.

After data are collected in a table, determine how many columns of differences are required to obtain a column of constant differences.

		1st diff.	2nd diff.
0	1		
		> 3	
1	4		> 4
		> 7	
2	11		> 4
		> 11	
3	22		> 4
		> 15	
4	37		> 4
		> 19	
5	56		
n	?		

In the example, note that it takes two columns of differences to obtain constants.

The numbers in the first column of differences are 3, 7, 11, 15, and 19. Since these are not constant, create a second column of differences. The differences between these numbers *are* constant, since each difference is 4.

It may be necessary to create several columns of differences to find a constant difference. Once the constant difference has been found, use the formulas in the Finite Difference Chart. Note that there are four tables of formulas on this chart. The chart shows that every first degree expression has only one column of differences; every second degree expression has two columns of differences, etc. The choice of table is determined by how many columns of differences are required to generate a constant difference. For example, if only one column is required, the solution may be found through the first degree table. If three columns are required, the third degree table would be used.

In the earlier example, two columns of differences are required to reach a constant difference so the solution is available through the second degree table. To solve this problem, assign the values in the problem's table to the corresponding expressions in the Finite Difference Chart for second degree expressions.

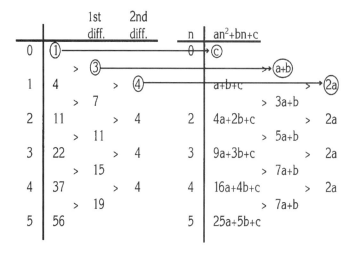

Assigning these values creates the following three equations:

$$c = 1$$
$$a + b = 3$$
$$2a = 4$$

Solving these three equations, beginning with $2a = 4$, produces the following values for a, b, and c.

$$a = 2$$
$$b = 1$$
$$c = 1$$

When these values are substituted in the general second degree expression, $an^2 + bn + c$, the result is $2n^2 + n + 1$, the general formula for the horizontal solution.

While the method of finite differences is frequently a very convenient problem solving approach, it will not always lead to a solution (constant differences may not occur), nor is it necessarily the best way to approach a problem.

The Finite Difference Chart may be especially useful if students are challenged to discover how the chart is constructed and to experiment with the technique on problems which may have been solved through other processes.

FINITE DIFFERENCE CHART

First Degree

n	an+b
0	b
1	a+b
2	2a+b
3	3a+b
4	4a+b
5	5a+b

(differences: a, a, a, a, a)

Second Degree

n	an²+bn+c
0	c
1	a+b+c
2	4a+2b+c
3	9a+3b+c
4	16a+4b+c
5	25a+5b+c

(first differences: a+b, 3a+b, 5a+b, 7a+b, 9a+b; second differences: 2a, 2a, 2a, 2a)

Third Degree

n	an³+bn²+cn+d
0	d
1	a+b+c+d
2	8a+4b+2c+d
3	27a+9b+3c+d
4	64a+16b+4c+d
5	125a+26b+5c+d

(first differences: a+b+c, 7a+3b+c, 19a+5b+c, 37a+7b+c, 61a+9b+c; second differences: 6a+2b, 12a+2b, 18a+2b, 24a+2b; third differences: 6a, 6a, 6a)

Fourth Degree

n	an⁴+bn³+cn²+dn+e
0	e
1	a+b+c+d+e
2	16a+8d+4c+2d+e
3	81a+27b+9c+3d+e
4	256a+64b+16c+4d+e
5	625a+125b+25c+5d+e
6	1296a+216b+36c+6d+e

(first differences: a+b+c+d, 15a+7b+3c+d, 65a+19b+5c+d, 175a+37b+7c+d, 369a+61b+9c+d, 671a+91b+11c+d; second differences: 14a+6b+2c, 50a+12b+2c, 110a+18b+2c, 194a+24b+2c, 302a+30b+2c; third differences: 36a+6b, 60a+6b, 84a+6b, 108a+6b; fourth differences: 24a, 24a, 24a)

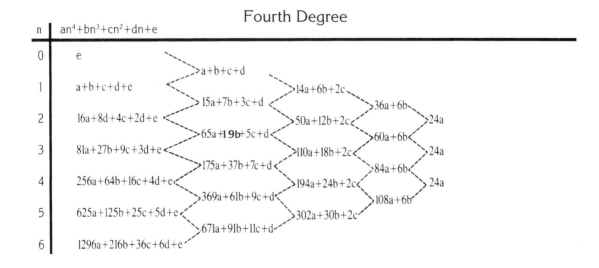

SAMPLE SPACE FOR TOSSING THREE DICE

1	1	1	2	4	1	4	1	1	5	4	1
1	1	2	2	4	2	4	1	2	5	4	2
1	1	3	2	4	3	4	1	3	5	4	3
1	1	4	2	4	4	4	1	4	5	4	4
1	1	5	2	4	5	4	1	5	5	4	5
1	1	6	2	4	6	4	1	6	5	4	6
1	2	1	2	5	1	4	2	1	5	5	1
1	2	2	2	5	2	4	2	2	5	5	2
1	2	3	2	5	3	4	2	3	5	5	3
1	2	4	2	5	4	4	2	4	5	5	4
1	2	5	2	5	5	4	2	5	5	5	5
1	2	6	2	5	6	4	2	6	5	5	6
1	3	1	2	6	1	4	3	1	5	6	1
1	3	2	2	6	2	4	3	2	5	6	2
1	3	3	2	6	3	4	3	3	5	6	3
1	3	4	2	6	4	4	3	4	5	6	4
1	3	5	2	6	5	4	3	5	5	6	5
1	3	6	2	6	6	4	3	6	5	6	6
1	4	1	3	1	1	4	4	1	6	1	1
1	4	2	3	1	2	4	4	2	6	1	2
1	4	3	3	1	3	4	4	3	6	1	3
1	4	4	3	1	4	4	4	4	6	1	4
1	4	5	3	1	5	4	4	5	6	1	5
1	4	6	3	1	6	4	4	6	6	1	6
1	5	1	3	2	1	4	5	1	6	2	1
1	5	2	3	2	2	4	5	2	6	2	2
1	5	3	3	2	3	4	5	3	6	2	3
1	5	4	3	2	4	4	5	4	6	2	4
1	5	5	3	2	5	4	5	5	6	2	5
1	5	6	3	2	6	4	5	6	6	2	6
1	6	1	3	3	1	4	6	1	6	3	1
1	6	2	3	3	2	4	6	2	6	3	2
1	6	3	3	3	3	4	6	3	6	3	3
1	6	4	3	3	4	4	6	4	6	3	4
1	6	5	3	3	5	4	6	5	6	3	5
1	6	6	3	3	6	4	6	6	6	3	6
2	1	1	3	4	1	5	1	1	6	4	1
2	1	2	3	4	2	5	1	2	6	4	2
2	1	3	3	4	3	5	1	3	6	4	3
2	1	4	3	4	4	5	1	4	6	4	4
2	1	5	3	4	5	5	1	5	6	4	5
2	1	6	3	4	6	5	1	6	6	4	6
2	2	1	3	5	1	5	2	1	6	5	1
2	2	2	3	5	2	5	2	2	6	5	2
2	2	3	3	5	3	5	2	3	6	5	3
2	2	4	3	5	4	5	2	4	6	5	4
2	2	5	3	5	5	5	2	5	6	5	5
2	2	6	3	5	6	5	2	6	6	5	6
2	3	1	3	6	1	5	3	1	6	6	1
2	3	2	3	6	2	5	3	2	6	6	2
2	3	3	3	6	3	5	3	3	6	6	3
2	3	4	3	6	4	5	3	4	6	6	4
2	3	5	3	6	5	5	3	5	6	6	5
2	3	6	3	6	6	5	3	6	6	6	6

SOLUTIONS

WHAT'S MISSING?
(pg. 1)

1. Two, four, six, eight, ten, twelve, fourteen
2. One, three, two, four, three, five, four, six
3. 3, 6, 9, 12, 15, 18
4. a, b, d, g, k, p, v
5. 10, 8, 14, 12, 18, 16, 22, 20, 26
6. z, x, v, t, r, p, n
7. 1, 3, 6, 10, 15, 21, 28

8.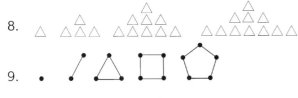

9.

10.

11.

12.

FOLLOW THE ORDERS!
(pg. 2)

1. (1,2),(3,4),(5,6),(0,1),(10,11),(2,3),(6,7),(8,9)
2. (2,4),(6,12),(3,6),(4,8),(13,26),(5,10)
3. (9,3),(3,1),(12,4),(6,2),(15,5),(24,8)
4. (1,3),(7,9),(3,5),(8,10),(16,18),(11,13),(6,8)
5. (4,0),(2,0),(9,0),(12,0),(6,0),(22,0)
6. (4,16),(7,49),(5,25),(8,64),(10,100),(6,36)
7. (4,9),(5,11),(2,5),(6,13),(3,7),(10,21),(1,3)
8. (10,2),(25,5),(5,1),(35,7),(50,10),(45,9),(15,3)
9. (24,3),(16,2),(40,5),(32,4),(56,7),(64,8)
10. (3,10),(6,37),(2,5),(7,50),(5,26),(1,2),(9,82)
11. (88,8),(44,4),(55,5),(11,1),(66,6),(110,10)
12. (12,8),(6,5),(10,7),(14,9),(20,12),(24,14),(100,52)

EXTRA CHALLENGES:
1. (3,6),(8,56),(5,20),(6,30),(10,90),(4,12)
2. (16,2),(64,4),(36,3),(100,5),(4,1),(144,6)

NAME THAT NUMBER!
(pg. 3)

1	5
2	7
3	9
4	11
5	13
6	15
50	103
n	2n+3

1	3
2	6
3	11
4	18
5	27
6	38
50	2502
n	$n^2 + 2$

1	7
2	10
3	13
4	16
5	19
6	22
50	154
n	3n+4

1	8
2	13
3	18
4	23
5	28
6	33
50	253
n	5n+3

1	1
2	5
3	9
4	13
5	17
6	21
50	197
n	4n-3

1	0
2	3
3	8
4	15
5	24
6	35
50	2499
n	$n^2 - 1$

FIGURE IT OUT
(pg. 4)

1. 302
2. 201
3. 204
4. 10000
5. 5352

EASY AS PIE!
(pg. 5)

Number of Cuts	Number of Pieces
1	2
2	4
3	6
4	8
5	10
6	12
7	14
8	16
9	18
10	20
20	40
n	2n

Additional Activity:
Some teachers may wish to suggest another pie cutting activity which requires that all the cuts be parallel.

The solution to this problem is shown.

Number of Parallel Cuts	Number of Pieces
1	2
2	3
3	4
4	5
5	6
n	n+1

A BANQUET AT TONY'S
(pg. 6)

Number of Tables	Number of People
1	4
2	6
3	8
4	10
5	12
6	14
7	16
8	18
30	62
n	2n+2

THREE FOR ME
(pg.7)

Triple Pattern #1

(1, 3, 6)
(4, 12, 24)
(5, 15, 30)
(10, 30, 60)
(6, 18, 36)
(7, 21, 42)

Triple Pattern #2

(1, 3, 6)
(5, 7, 10)
(19, 21, 24)
(8, 10, 13)
(31, 33, 36)
(15, 17, 20)
(45, 47, 50)
(49, 51, 54)
(88, 90, 93)

Triple Pattern #3

(1, 5, 10)
(2, 6, 12)
(8, 12, 24)
(6, 10, 20)
(14, 18, 36)
(11, 15, 30)
(12, 16, 32)
(56, 60, 120)

Triple Pattern #4

(6, 36, 12)
(5, 30, 10)
(2, 12, 4)
(4, 24, 8)
(3, 18, 6)
(10, 60, 20)
(7, 42, 14)
(11, 66, 22)

Triple Pattern #5

(2, 3, 10)
(3, 5, 16)
(4, 6, 20)
(6, 1, 14)
(5, 8, 26)
(1, 7, 16)
(8, 7, 30)
(10, 14, 48)
(8, 12, 40)

EXPOSED!
(pg.8)

Figure	Height in Squares	Number of Squares	Squares Exposed On			
			No Sides	1 Side	2 Sides	3 Sides
1	2	4	0	1	0	3
2	3	9	1	3	2	3
3	4	16	4	5	4	3
4	5	25	9	7	6	3
5	6	36	16	9	8	3
n	n+1	$(n+1)^2$	$(n-1)^2$	2n-1	2n-2	3

ODD DENOMINATORS
(pg. 9)

Number of Terms	Sum
1	$\frac{1}{3}$
2	$\frac{2}{5}$
3	$\frac{3}{7}$
4	$\frac{4}{9}$
5	$\frac{5}{11}$
6	$\frac{6}{13}$
7	$\frac{7}{15}$
50	$\frac{50}{101}$

Extra Challenge Solution: $\frac{n}{2n+1}$

FROM FRACTIONS TO DECIMALS
(pg. 10)

a. .44444444444444444444
b. .30303030303030303030
c. .07692307692307692307
d. .02702702702702702702
e. .03703703703703703703
f. .02439024390243902439
g. .18918918918918918918
h. .30030030030030030030

CRISS-CROSSED SUMS
(pg. 11)

Entries in tables will vary as students select crosses. In each case the sum of the five numbers in the cross will be five times the center number.

UP AND COMING TRIANGLES
(pg. 12)

Side Measurement	Number of Triangles Pointing Up
1	1
2	4
3	10
4	20
5	35
6	56
7	84
8	120

In this activity, count only those triangles which point up. For example, when the side measurement is three, there are six triangles with one unit sides, three triangles with two unit sides and one triangle with three unit sides for a total of 10 triangles pointing up.

The first set of differences for the numbers in the second column is 1, 3, 6, 10, 15, etc.—the triangular numbers. The second set of differences is 1, 2, 3, 4, etc. This discovery allows the second column to be continued indefinitely.

Note: The numbers in the second column also appear in the fourth diagonal of Pascal's triangle (see Appendix).

Extra Challenge Solution: $\frac{n^3+3n^2+2n}{6}$

The horizontal solution for this problem may be obtained using the method of finite differences (see Appendix).

Another approach is to give students some help by asking them to examine the following:
$1 \cdot 2 \cdot 3 = 6$
$2 \cdot 3 \cdot 4 = 24$
$3 \cdot 4 \cdot 5 = 60$
$4 \cdot 5 \cdot 6 = 120$
etc.
The products are always six times the numbers in the second column. From this we reach the solution $\frac{n(n+1)(n+2)}{6}$ which is algebraically equal to $\frac{n^3+3n^2+2n}{6}$.

SIDE BY SIDE
(pg. 13)

Triangle	Length of Side	Number of Triangles	Number of Triangles Exposed On		
			No Sides	1 Side	2 Sides
1	2	4	1	0	3
2	3	9	3	3	3
3	4	16	7	6	3
4	5	25	13	9	3
5	6	36	21	12	3
6	7	49	31	15	3
n	n+1	$(n+1)^2$	$n(n-1)+1$ or n^2-n+1	$3n-3$	3

WHAT'S YOUR ANGLE?
(pg. 14)

Number of Rays	Total Number of Angles
2	1
3	3
4	6
5	10
6	15
7	21
8	28
9	36
10	45

Extra Challenge Solution: $\dfrac{n(n-1)}{2}$

NUMBER 999 IS A FRIEND OF MINE
(pg. 15)

999 • 121 = 120,879   999 • 146 = 145,854
999 • 237 = 236,763   999 • 257 = 256,743
999 • 312 = 311,688   999 • 343 = 342,657
999 • 369 = 368,631   999 • 445 = 444,555
999 • 426 = 425,574   999 • 674 = 673,326
999 • 576 = 575,424   999 • 712 = 711,288
999 • 643 = 642,357   999 • 999 = 998,001
999 • 790 = 789,210
999 • 834 = 833,166
999 • 900 = 899,100

The key to these products is that the first three digits of the answer is one less than the number multiplied times 999. The last three digits of the answer are obtained by seeing that the sum of the first three digits and the last three digits is always 999.

ARRAYS THAT AMAZE!
(pg. 16)

One helpful hint for finding the horizontal solution is to subtract one from each number in the second column. The resulting numbers can be obtained by taking the number in the first column and multiplying it by a number one less.

Row Number	Middle Number
1	1
2	3
3	7
4	13
5	21
50	2451
n	n(n-1)+1

Extra Challenge: 400 is a square number. Observe that the numbers on the far right diagonal are squares. The number under any square is one less than the next square. Therefore, the number directly under 400 is 441 -1 = 440.

WHAT'S HAPPENIN'?
(pg. 17)

H	H	H	H
H	H	H	T
H	H	T	H
H	H	T	T
H	T	H	H
H	T	H	T
H	T	T	H
H	T	T	T
T	H	H	H
T	H	H	T
T	H	T	H
T	H	T	T
T	T	H	H
T	T	H	T
T	T	T	H
T	T	T	T

H	H	H	H	H
H	H	H	H	T
H	H	H	T	H
H	H	H	T	T
H	H	T	H	H
H	H	T	H	T
H	H	T	T	H
H	H	T	T	T
H	T	H	H	H
H	T	H	H	T
H	T	H	T	H
H	T	H	T	T
H	T	T	H	H
H	T	T	H	T
H	T	T	T	H
H	T	T	T	T
T	H	H	H	H
T	H	H	H	T
T	H	H	T	H
T	H	H	T	T
T	H	T	H	H
T	H	T	H	T
T	H	T	T	H
T	H	T	T	T
T	T	H	H	H
T	T	H	H	T
T	T	H	T	H
T	T	H	T	T
T	T	T	H	H
T	T	T	H	T
T	T	T	T	H
T	T	T	T	T

FLIP FOR IT!
(pg. 18)

Note that the numerators for each row may be found in a row in Pascal's triangle (see Appendix) and the denominator is the sum of the numbers in that row.

Number of Coins	Probability of Tossing Exactly						
	0 Heads	1 Head	2 Heads	3 Heads	4 Heads	5 Heads	6 Heads
1	$\frac{1}{2}$	$\frac{1}{2}$					
2	$\frac{1}{4}$	$\frac{2}{4}$	$\frac{1}{4}$				
3	$\frac{1}{8}$	$\frac{3}{8}$	$\frac{3}{8}$	$\frac{1}{8}$			
4	$\frac{1}{16}$	$\frac{4}{16}$	$\frac{6}{16}$	$\frac{4}{16}$	$\frac{1}{16}$		
5	$\frac{1}{32}$	$\frac{5}{32}$	$\frac{10}{32}$	$\frac{10}{32}$	$\frac{5}{32}$	$\frac{1}{32}$	
6	$\frac{1}{64}$	$\frac{6}{64}$	$\frac{15}{64}$	$\frac{20}{64}$	$\frac{15}{64}$	$\frac{6}{64}$	$\frac{1}{64}$

From the table we see that when six coins are tossed the probability of getting exactly three heads is $\frac{20}{64} = \frac{5}{16} = 31.25\%$.

TOSS FOR TRIANGLES
(pg. 19)

The sample space when three dice are tossed contains 216 possibilities. One part of this activity is to have students construct the sample space begun in the activity, discovering patterns which would be helpful in its construction.

Some students may need help to complete the sample space. Comparing the process to the workings of an odometer on a car may help. The problem uses {1,2,3,4,5,6} instead of {0,1,2,3,4,5,6,7,8,9} as an odometer does.

If teachers prefer, they may photocopy this rather lengthy sample space (provided in the Appendix). Ask students to determine how many of the 216 possibilities produce triangles. The answer is 111. When tossing three dice, the probability of obtaining values which could be used as lengths of sides of a triangle is $\frac{111}{216} = 51.4\%$.

Extra Challenge:

It is strongly suggested that teachers encourage students to collect experimental values to compare with this theoretical value. Divide students into small groups and pool results to quickly collect experimental results for 1000 or more tosses. With this many tosses the experimental results should be quite close to the theoretical.

Additional Activities:
A. Using the sample space for three dice, students may be asked to determine the probability, when three dice are tossed, of obtaining
   1. an equilateral triangle (6/216).
   2. an isosceles triangle (exactly two sides equal) (63/216).
   3. a scalene triangle (42/216).

B. The Three Dice Triangle Game

For practice with determining results from tossing dice in this manner, a game can be devised. While not strictly following the probabilities but still paying attention to them, the following point scoring system is one of many that could be used:

   Roll three dice:
   If a scalene triangle can be formed, score 3 points.
   If an isosceles triangle can be formed, score 2 points.
   If an equilateral triangle can be formed, score 10 points.
   If no triangle can be formed, deduct 1 point.

Players take turns and keep a running score. The first to score a given total, say 20 or 25 points, is the winner. This is an activity that helps students learn about triangles and how to classify them by their sides.

BLOCK BLITZ
(pg. 20)

Number of Structures	Total Number of Blocks
1	1
2	9
3	36
4	100
5	225
6	441
7	784
8	1296

Extra Challenge: The total number of blocks is always the square of a triangular number.
For 20 structures the solution is $\left[\frac{(20)(21)}{2}\right]^2 = 44,100$.

For n structures the solution is $\left[\frac{n(n+1)}{2}\right]^2$.

ROWING WITH PASCAL
(pg. 21)

Row Number	Sum
1	1
2	2
3	4
4	8
5	16
6	32
7	64
8	128
9	256
10	512

Extra Challenge
Solution: 2^{n-1}

ABOVE AVERAGE
(pg. 22)

A.

Number of Terms	Average
2	2
3	3
4	4
5	5
6	6
50	50

B.

Number of Terms	Average
2	7
3	8
4	9
5	10
6	11
50	55

C.

Number of Terms	Average
2	$1\frac{1}{2}$
3	2
4	$2\frac{1}{2}$
5	3
6	$3\frac{1}{2}$
50	$25\frac{1}{2}$

D.

Number of Terms	Average
2	6
3	8
4	10
5	12
6	14
50	102

MAGIC SQUARES
(pg. 23)

This activity is designed to be the first in the study of magic squares. Before students are shown the general method for constructing odd by odd magic squares, let them try this activity by trial and error. Be sure that each row, each column, and each diagonal adds up to 15.

Solutions students come up with may be reflections of the one shown.

8	1	6
3	5	7
4	9	2

MAKING MAGIC SQUARES
(pg. 24)

17	24	1	8	15
23	5	7	14	16
4	6	13	20	22
10	12	19	21	3
11	18	25	2	9

30	39	48	1	10	19	28
38	47	7	9	18	27	29
46	6	8	17	26	35	37
5	14	16	25	34	36	45
13	15	24	33	42	44	4
21	23	32	41	43	3	12
22	31	40	49	2	11	20

MAGIC SQUARE MADNESS
(pg. 25)

31	3	23
11	19	27
15	35	7

19	5	15
9	13	17
11	21	7

45	10	35
20	30	40
25	50	15

34	48	2	16	30
46	10	14	28	32
8	12	26	40	44
20	24	38	42	6
22	36	50	4	18

59	77	95	1	19	37	55
75	93	13	17	35	53	57
91	11	15	33	51	69	73
9	27	31	49	67	71	89
25	29	47	65	83	87	7
41	45	63	81	85	5	23
43	61	79	97	3	21	39

MAGIC SQUARE DISCOVERIES
(pg. 26)

$$M = \frac{F + L}{2}$$

$$S = MD$$

$$L = F + (D^2 - 1)I$$

$$S = MD = \left[\left(\frac{F+L}{2}\right)D\right] = \left[\frac{F+F+(D^2-1)I}{2}\right]D = \frac{2FD+D^3I-DI}{2}$$

A MAGIC COMPOSITION
(pg. 27)

The key to making this composite magic square is to fill the 3 by 3 squares in the same order as you enter the numbers in the first 3 by 3 square.

71	64	69	8	1	6	53	46	51
66	68	70	3	5	7	48	50	52
67	72	65	4	9	2	49	54	47
26	19	24	44	37	42	62	55	60
21	23	25	39	41	43	57	59	61
22	27	20	40	45	38	58	63	56
35	28	33	80	73	78	17	10	15
30	32	34	75	77	79	12	14	16
30	36	29	76	81	74	13	18	11

THE ACE CASE
(pg. 28)

Sample Space

1 and 2	2 and 6
1 and 3	3 and 4
1 and 4	3 and 5
1 and 5	3 and 6
1 and 6	4 and 5
2 and 3	4 and 6
2 and 4	5 and 6
2 and 5	

Probability of picking at least one ace $= \frac{9}{15}$ or $\frac{3}{5}$ (60%).

Probability of picking no aces $= \frac{2}{5}$ (40%).

RINGS OF CIRCLES
(pg. 29)

Number of Rings	Total Number of Circles
0	1
1	7
2	19
3	37
4	61
5	91
6	127
7	169
8	217

The first set of differences for the numbers in the second column is 6, 12, 18, 24,... Using this pattern, the table can be extended indefinitely.

Extra Challenge
Solution: $3n^2 + 3n + 1$
The horizontal solution for this problem may be found using the method of finite differences (see Appendix).

Another approach teachers might suggest is to subtract one from each number in the second column. The resulting numbers are divisible by six. Dividing by six will produce the triangular numbers.

PATH PATTERNS
(pg. 30)

The pattern in this problem resembles the famous Fibonacci sequence 1, 1, 2, 3, 5, 8, 13, 21,... where each term is obtained by adding the two previous terms.

Dimensions	Number of Arrangements
2 by 1	1
2 by 2	2
2 by 3	3
2 by 4	5 (not 4)
2 by 5	8
2 by 6	13
2 by 7	21
2 by 8	34
2 by 9	55
2 by 10	89

FIFTY TERM SUM-UP
(pg. 31)

Extra Challenge
Solution: $2n(n+1)$

Number of Terms	Sum
1	4
2	12
3	24
4	40
5	60
6	84
7	112
50	5100

PRODUCT PATTERNS
(pg. 32)

The last two digits are the product of the units digits of the two given numbers. All but the last two digits are obtained by multiplying the tens digit by a number one larger.

THE HARMONIC TRIANGLE
(pg. 33)

When the denominators are divided by the row number, Pascal's triangle (see Appendix) emerges.

Many patterns may be discovered in the harmonic triangle. Several are included here:

1. The left and right-hand edges consist of the reciprocals of the positive integers. These are called harmonic numbers.
2. The denominators in the second diagonal (2, 6, 12, 20, 30,...) increase by 4, 6, 8, 10, etc.
3. All denominators in the second diagonal are divisible by 2. Dividing these denominators by 2 results in 1, 3, 6, 10,..., the triangular numbers.
4. All denominators in the third diagonal are divisible by 3, the fourth diagonal by 4, etc.
5. Each number in the harmonic triangle is the sum of the two fractions closest to it in the next row.
   For example,

$$\frac{1}{3} = \frac{1}{4} + \frac{1}{12} \text{ and } \frac{1}{12} = \frac{1}{20} + \frac{1}{30}$$

6. The sum of the numbers in any diagonal is equal to the first number in the previous diagonal minus the number directly to the left.
   For example,

$$\frac{1}{2} + \frac{1}{6} + \frac{1}{12} = \frac{1}{1} - \frac{1}{4} = \frac{3}{4}$$

$$\frac{1}{3} + \frac{1}{12} + \frac{1}{30} + \frac{1}{60} = \frac{1}{2} - \frac{1}{30} = \frac{7}{15}$$

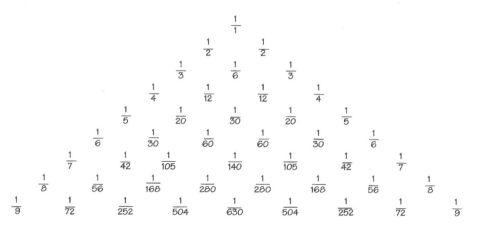

DO YOU HAVE CHANGE?
(pg. 34)

There are 49 ways you can make change for a half-dollar.

Extra Challenge: Constructing a similar table will show that there are 291 ways to make change for a dollar using pennies, nickels, dimes, quarters, and half-dollars.

Number	Quarters	Dimes	Nickels	Pennies
1	2	0	0	0
2	1	2	1	0
3	1	2	0	5
4	1	1	3	0
5	1	1	2	5
6	1	1	1	10
7	1	1	0	15
8	1	0	5	0
9	1	0	4	5
10	1	0	3	10
11	1	0	2	15
12	1	0	1	20
13	1	0	0	25
14	0	5	0	0
15	0	4	2	0
16	0	4	1	5
17	0	4	0	10
18	0	3	4	0
19	0	3	3	5
20	0	3	2	10
21	0	3	1	15
22	0	3	0	20
23	0	2	6	0
24	0	2	5	5
25	0	2	4	10
26	0	2	3	15
27	0	2	2	20
28	0	2	1	25
29	0	2	0	30
30	0	1	8	0
31	0	1	7	5
32	0	1	6	10
33	0	1	5	15
34	0	1	4	20
35	0	1	3	25
36	0	1	2	30
37	0	1	1	35
38	0	1	0	40
39	0	0	10	0
40	0	0	9	5
41	0	0	8	10
42	0	0	7	15
43	0	0	6	20
44	0	0	5	25
45	0	0	4	30
46	0	0	3	35
47	0	0	2	40
48	0	0	1	45
49	0	0	0	50

FIGURATIVE FAMILIES
(pg. 35)

Rank of Family Members

Family	1st	2nd	3rd	4th	5th	6th	7th	8th
Triangular	1	3	6	10	15	21	28	36
Square	1	4	9	16	25	36	49	64
Pentagonal	1	5	12	22	35	51	70	92
Hexagonal	1	6	15	28	45	66	91	120
Heptagonal	1	7	18	34	55	81	112	148
Octagonal	1	8	21	40	65	96	133	176

THE FLIP SIDE
(pg. 36)

Number of Terms	Sum
1	$\frac{1}{1}$
2	$\frac{4}{3}$
3	$\frac{3}{2}$
4	$\frac{8}{5}$
5	$\frac{5}{3}$
6	$\frac{12}{7}$
7	$\frac{7}{4}$
8	$\frac{16}{9}$
9	$\frac{9}{5}$
10	$\frac{20}{11}$

1. When the number in the left column is odd, the numerator is the same as the number in the left column. To find the denominator, increase the number in the left column by one, then divide by two.
2. When the number in the left column is even, the numerator is two times the number in the left column. The denominator is one more than the number in the left column.

3. (a) $\frac{160}{81}$ (b) $\frac{127}{64}$ (c) $\frac{2000}{1001}$

4. 2

WHITE-FACED CUBES
(pg. 37)

A model such as a Rubik's cube may help students visualize this problem. In this activity, students often begin thinking inductively (looking for the vertical pattern in each column) and then suddenly switch to deductive thinking by noticing where the various smaller cubes are located on the big cube–on an edge, in the middle of a face, on a corner, etc.

Length of Edge	Number of Cubes Formed	Number with 3 White Faces	Number with 2 White Faces	Number with 1 White Face	Number with No White Faces
2	8	8	0	0	0
3	27	8	12	6	1
4	64	8	24	24	8
5	125	8	36	54	27
6	216	8	48	96	64
20	8000	8	216	1944	5832
n	n^3	8	$12(n-2)$	$6(n-2)^2$	$(n-2)^3$

CHECKERBOARD CHALLENGE
(pg. 38)

Dimension of Board	Number of Squares
1 by 1	1
2 by 2	5
3 by 3	14
4 by 4	30
5 by 5	55
6 by 6	91
7 by 7	140
8 by 8	204

This activity requires that students count all squares on the boards. For example, the 3 by 3 board contains nine squares with one unit sides, four squares with two unit sides and one square with three unit sides for a total of 14.

The differences for the numbers in the second column are 4, 9, 16, 25, 36, ..., the square numbers. Using this pattern, the table can be extended indefinitely.

A MATTER OF DEGREES
(pg. 39)

Number of Sides	Number of Diagonals from One Vertex	Number of Triangles Made	Sum of Interior Angles
3	0	1	180°
4	1	2	360°
5	2	3	540°
6	3	4	720°
7	4	5	900°
8	5	6	1080°
n	n-3	n-2	180(n-2)°

THE SNOWFLAKE CURVE
(pg. 40)

As the snowflake "grows," the perimeter becomes infinitely large whereas the area approaches a finite quantity.

Solutions:

Stage Number	Number of Sides	Length of Each Side (in inches)
1	3	1
2	12	$\frac{1}{3}$
3	48	$\frac{1}{9}$
4	192	$\frac{1}{27}$
5	768	$\frac{1}{81}$
n	$3 \cdot 4^{n-1}$	$\frac{1}{3^{n-1}}$

Some students may need help creating the formulas for the nth stage. Teachers may give appropriate hints such as "Divide each number in the 'Number of Sides' column by 3." The resulting numbers are powers of 4.

The perimeter may be found by multiplying the number of sides times the length of each side.

$$P(n) = \frac{3 \cdot 4^{n-1}}{3^{n-1}} = \frac{4^{n-1}}{3^{n-2}}$$

$$P(60) = \frac{4^{59}}{3^{58}} \text{ inches } = 1114 \text{ miles}$$

$$P(100) = \frac{4^{99}}{3^{98}} \text{ inches } = 110,723,807 \text{ miles.}$$

For a dramatic classroom presentation, show the snowflake curve being drawn on a computer screen. Enter the following Apple Logo programs for the snowflake curve.

```
TO SIDE :SIZE :STAGE
IF :STAGE = 1 [FD :SIZE STOP]
SIDE :SIZE/3 :STAGE -1
LT 60
SIDE :SIZE/3 :STAGE -1
RT 120
SIDE :SIZE/3 :STAGE -1
LT 60
SIDE :SIZE/3 :STAGE -1
END

TO SN :STAGE
MAKE "SIZE 180
PU SETPOS [-50 -75]
PD
REPEAT 3[SIDE :SIZE :STAGE RT 120]
END
```

To run the program, enter SN followed by a number which indicates the stage to be drawn. For example, when SN 1 is entered, the turtle will draw stage 1 of the snowflake curve. When SN 2 is entered, stage 2 is drawn, etc. Draw several stages, clearing the screen (CS) between drawings.

REPEATING RECTANGLES
(pg. 41)

Figure	Number of Rectangles
1	4
2	7
3	10
4	13
5	16
6	19
7	22
50	151
n	3n+1

KNIGHT PAIRS ON THE CHESSBOARD
(pg. 42)

Encourage students to be orderly in listing the knight pairs. For the 3 by 3 board the list might look like this:

A and H   C and D
A and F   C and H
B and G   D and I
B and I   F and G

Once the data have been collected for the 3 by 3, 4 by 4, and 5 by 5 boards, look for a pattern. Dividing the numbers in the second column by 8 results in the triangular numbers. This can be used to find the general formula.

Size of Board	Number of Knight Pairs
3 by 3	8
4 by 4	24
5 by 5	48
6 by 6	80
7 by 7	120
8 by 8	168
n by n	$4n^2-12n+8$

DIAGONAL CHALLENGE
(pg. 43)

Number of Sides	Number of Diagonals
3	0
4	2
5	5
6	9
7	14
8	20
9	27
10	35

Extra Challenge
Solution: $\dfrac{n(n-3)}{2}$

REGION REVENGE
(pg. 44)

This is a classic mathematical problem which has intrigued students for years. The numbers in the second column will surprise students in that the pattern goes 1, 2, 4, 8, 16, 31— not 32. Remind students to check differences to complete the table. The first set of differences for the numbers in the second column is 1, 2, 4, 8, 15, ..., the second set of differences is 1, 2, 4, 7, ..., the third set of differences is 1, 2, 3, ..., allowing students to continue the table. indefinitely.

Number of Points	Maximum Number of Regions
1	1
2	2
3	4
4	8
5	16
6	31 (not 32)
7	57
8	99
9	163
10	256

Extra Challenge Solution : $\dfrac{n^4-6n^3+23n^2-18n+24}{24}$

The method of finite differences (see Appendix) is the easiest way to find the horizontal solution to this problem.

Since four columns of differences are required to obtain constants, the solution will be a fourth degree expression.

Number of Points	Maximum Number of Regions	1st Diff.	2nd Diff.	3rd Diff.	4th Diff.
1	1				
		1			
2	2		1		
		2		1	
3	4		2		1
		4		2	
4	8		4		1
		8		3	
5	16		7		1
		15		4	
6	31		11		
		26			
7	57				

To solve the problem, assign the values in the problem to the corresponding formulas outlined on the finite difference chart (see Appendix). This is shown below.

$a+b+c+d+e = 1$ $60a+6b = 1$
$15a+7b+3c+d = 1$ $24a = 1$
$50a+12b+2c = 1$

Solving these five equations, beginning with $24a = 1$, produces the following values for a, b, c, d, and e.

$a = \dfrac{1}{24}$ $d = \dfrac{-18}{24}$

$b = \dfrac{-6}{24}$ $e = 1$ or $\dfrac{24}{24}$

$c = \dfrac{23}{24}$

Substituting these values in the general fourth degree expression, $an^4+ bn^3+ cn^2+ dn + e$, gives the horizontal solution: $\dfrac{n^4-6n^3+23n^2-18n+24}{24}$.

AIMS Duplication Rights Program

AIMS has received many requests from school districts for the purchase of unlimited duplication rights to AIMS materials. In response, the AIMS Education Foundation has formulated the program outlined below. There is a built-in flexibility which, we trust, will provide for those who use AIMS materials extensively to purchase such rights for either individual activities or entire books.

It is the goal of the AIMS Education Foundation to make its materials and programs available at reasonable cost. All income from the sale of publications and duplication rights is used to support AIMS programs; hence, strict adherence to regulations governing duplication is essential. Duplication of AIMS materials beyond limits set by copyright laws and those specified below is strictly forbidden.

Limited Duplication Rights

Any purchaser of an AIMS book may make up to *200 copies* of any activity in that book for use at *one school site*. Beyond that, rights must be purchased according to the appropriate category.

Unlimited Duplication Rights for Single Activities

An individual or school may purchase the right to make an unlimited number of copies of a single activity. The royalty is $5.00 per activity per school site.

Examples: 3 activities x 1 site x $5.00 = $15.00
9 activities x 3 sites x $5.00 = $135.00

Unlimited Duplication Rights for Entire Books

A school or district may purchase the right to make an unlimited number of copies of a single, *specified* book. The royalty is $20.00 per book per school site. This is in addition to the cost of the book.

Examples: 5 books x 1 site   x $20.00 = $100.00
12 books x 10 sites x $20.00 = $2400.00

Magazine/Newsletter Duplication Rights

Members of the AIMS Education Foundation who purchase the *AIMS* magazine/*Newsletter* are hereby granted permission to make up to 200 copies of any portion of it, provided these copies will be used for educational purposes.

Workshop Instructors' Duplication Rights

Workshop instructors may distribute to registered workshop participants a maximum of 100 copies of any article and/or 100 copies of no more than eight activities, provided these six conditions are met:

1. Since all AIMS activities are based upon the *AIMS Model of Mathematics* and the *AIMS Model of Learning*, leaders must include in their presentations an explanation of these two models.
2. Workshop instructors must relate the AIMS activities presented to these basic explanations of the AIMS philosophy of education.
3. The copyright notice must appear on all materials distributed.
4. Instructors must provide information enabling participants to apply for membership in the AIMS Education Foundation or order books from the Foundation.
5. Instructors must inform participants of their limited duplication rights as outlined below.
6. Only student pages may be duplicated.

Written permission must be obtained for duplication beyond the limits listed above. Additional royalty payments may be required.

Workshop Participants' Rights

Those enrolled in workshops in which AIMS student activity sheets are distributed may duplicate a maximum of 35 copies or enough to use the lessons one time with one class, whichever is less. Beyond that, rights must be purchased according to the appropriate category.

Application for Duplication Rights

The purchasing agency or individual must clearly specify the following:
1. Name, address, and telephone number
2. Titles of the books for Unlimited Duplication Rights contracts
3. Titles of activities for Unlimited Duplication Rights contracts
4. Names and addresses of school sites for which duplication rights are being purchased.

NOTE: Books to be duplicated must be purchased separately and are not included in the contract for Unlimited Duplication Rights.

The requested duplication rights are automatically authorized when proper payment is received, although a *Certificate of Duplication Rights* will be issued when the application is processed.

Address all correspondence to: **Contract Division**
AIMS Education Foundation
P.O. Box 8120
Fresno, CA 93747-8120

We invite you to subscribe to $\mathcal{AIMS}$!

Each issue of $\mathcal{AIMS}$ contains a variety of material useful to educators at all grade levels. Feature articles of lasting value deal with topics such as mathematical or science concepts, curriculum, assessment, the teaching of process skills, and historical background. Several of the latest AIMS math/science investigations are always included, along with their reproducible activity sheets. As needs direct and space allows, various issues contain news of current developments, such as workshop schedules, activities of the AIMS Instructional Leadership Network, and announcements of upcoming publications.

$\mathcal{AIMS}$ is published monthly, August through May. Subscriptions are on an annual basis only. A subscription entered at any time will begin with the next issue, but will also include the previous issues of that volume. Readers have preferred this arrangement because articles and activities within an annual volume are often interrelated.

Please note that an $\mathcal{AIMS}$ subscription automatically includes duplication rights for one school site for all issues included in the subscription. Many schools build cost-effective library resources with their subscriptions.

YES! I am interested in subscribing to $\mathcal{AIMS}$.

Name _____   Home Phone _____

Address _____   City, State, Zip _____

Please send the following volumes (subject to availability):

_____	Volume V	(1990-91)	$30.00	_____	Volume X	(1995-96) $30.00
_____	Volume VI	(1991-92)	$30.00	_____	Volume XI	(1996-97) $30.00
_____	Volume VII	(1992-93)	$30.00	_____	Volume XII	(1997-98) $30.00
_____	Volume IX	(1994-95)	$30.00	_____	Volume XIII	(1998-99) $30.00

_____ **Limited offer: Volumes XIII & XIV (1998-2000) $55.00**
(Note: Prices may change without notice)

Check your method of payment:

❏ Check enclosed in the amount of $ _____

❏ Purchase order attached (Please include the P.O.#, the authorizing signature, and position of the authorizing person.)

❏ Credit Card   ❏ Visa   ❏ MasterCard   Amount $ _____

Card # _____   Expiration Date _____

Signature _____   Today's Date _____

Make checks payable to **AIMS Education Foundation**.
Mail to $\mathcal{AIMS}$ magazine, P.O. Box 8120, Fresno, CA 93747-8120.
Phone (209) 255-4094 or (888) 733-2467 FAX (209) 255-6396
AIMS Homepage: http://www.AIMSedu.org/

AIMS Program Publications

GRADES K-4 SERIES

Bats Incredible

Brinca de Alegria Hacia la Primavera con las Matemáticas y Ciencias

Cáete de Gusto Hacia el Otoño con la Matemáticas y Ciencias

Cycles of Knowing and Growing

Fall Into Math and Science

Field Detectives

Glide Into Winter With Math and Science

Hardhatting in a Geo-World (Revised Edition, 1996)

Jaw Breakers and Heart Thumpers (Revised Edition, 1995)

Los Cincos Sentidos

Overhead and Underfoot (Revised Edition, 1994)

Patine al Invierno con Matemáticas y Ciencias

Popping With Power (Revised Edition, 1996)

Primariamente Física (Revised Edition, 1994)

Primarily Earth

Primariamente Plantas

Primarily Physics (Revised Edition, 1994)

Primarily Plants

Sense-able Science

Spring Into Math and Science

Under Construction

GRADES K-6 SERIES

Budding Botanist

Critters

El Botanista Principiante

Mostly Magnets

Ositos Nada Más

Primarily Bears

Principalmente Imanes

Water Precious Water

GRADES 5-9 SERIES

Actions with Fractions

Brick Layers

Conexiones Eléctricas

Down to Earth

Electrical Connections

Finding Your Bearings (Revised Edition, 1996)

Floaters and Sinkers (Revised Edition, 1995)

From Head to Toe

Fun With Foods

Historical Connections in Mathematics, Volume I

Historical Connections in Mathematics, Volume II

Historical Connections in Mathematics, Volume III

Machine Shop

Magnificent Microworld Adventures

Math + Science, A Solution

Off the Wall Science: A Poster Series Revisited

Our Wonderful World

Out of This World (Revised Edition, 1994)

Pieces and Patterns, A Patchwork in Math and Science

Piezas y Diseños, un Mosaic de Matemáticas y Ciencias

Soap Films and Bubbles

Spatial Visualization

The Sky's the Limit (Revised Edition, 1994)

The Amazing Circle, Volume 1

Through the Eyes of the Explorers:
    Minds-on Math & Mapping

What's Next, Volume 1

What's Next, Volume 2

What's Next, Volume 3

For further information write to:

AIMS Education Foundation • P.O. Box 8120 • Fresno, California 93747-8120

The AIMS Program

AIMS is the acronym for "Activities Integrating Mathematics and Science." Such integration enriches learning and makes it meaningful and holistic. AIMS began as a project of Fresno Pacific University to integrate the study of mathematics and science in grades K-9, but has since expanded to include language arts, social studies, and other disciplines.

AIMS is a continuing program of the non-profit AIMS Education Foundation. It had its inception in a National Science Foundation funded program whose purpose was to explore the effectiveness of integrating mathematics and science. The project directors in cooperation with 80 elementary classroom teachers devoted two years to a thorough field-testing of the results and implications of integration.

The approach met with such positive results that the decision was made to launch a program to create instructional materials incorporating this concept. Despite the fact that thoughtful educators have long recommended an integrative approach, very little appropriate material was available in 1981 when the project began. A series of writing projects have ensued and today the AIMS Education Foundation is committed to continue the creation of new integrated activities on a permanent basis.

The AIMS program is funded through the sale of this developing series of books and proceeds from the Foundation's endowment. All net income from program and products flows into a trust fund administered by the AIMS Education Foundation. Use of these funds is restricted to support of research, development, and publication of new materials. Writers donate all their rights to the Foundation to support its on-going program. No royalties are paid to the writers.

The rationale for integration lies in the fact that science, mathematics, language arts, social studies, etc., are integrally interwoven in the real world from which it follows that they should be similarly treated in the classroom where we are preparing students to live in that world. Teachers who use the AIMS program give enthusiastic endorsement to the effectiveness of this approach.

Science encompasses the art of questioning, investigating, hypothesizing, discovering, and communicating. Mathematics is the language that provides clarity, objectivity, and understanding. The language arts provide us powerful tools of communication. Many of the major contemporary societal issues stem from advancements in science and must be studied in the context of the social sciences. Therefore, it is timely that all of us take seriously a more holistic mode of educating our students. This goal motivates all who are associated with the AIMS Program. We invite you to join us in this effort.

Meaningful integration of knowledge is a major recommendation coming from the nation's professional science and mathematics associations. The American Association for the Advancement of Science in *Science for All Americans* strongly recommends the integration of mathematics, science, and technology. The National Council of Teachers of Mathematics places strong emphasis on applications of mathematics such as are found in science investigations. AIMS is fully aligned with these recommendations.

Extensive field testing of AIMS investigations confirms these beneficial results.

1. Mathematics becomes more meaningful, hence more useful, when it is applied to situations that interest students.
2. The extent to which science is studied and understood is increased, with a significant economy of time, when mathematics and science are integrated.
3. There is improved quality of learning and retention, supporting the thesis that learning which is meaningful and relevant is more effective.
4. Motivation and involvement are increased dramatically as students investigate real-world situations and participate actively in the process.

We invite you to become part of this classroom teacher movement by using an integrated approach to learning and sharing any suggestions you may have. The AIMS Program welcomes you!

AIMS Education Foundation Programs

A Day with AIMS

Intensive one-day workshops are offered to introduce educators to the philosophy and rationale of AIMS. Participants will discuss the methodology of AIMS and the strategies by which AIMS principles may be incorporated into curriculum. Each participant will take part in a variety of hands-on AIMS investigations to gain an understanding of such aspects as the scientific/mathematical content, classroom management, and connections with other curricular areas. *A Day with AIMS* workshops may be offered anywhere in the United States. Necessary supplies and take-home materials are usually included in the enrollment fee.

A Week with AIMS

Throughout the nation, AIMS offers many one-week workshops each year, usually in the summer. Each workshop lasts five days and includes at least 30 hours of AIMS hands-on instruction. Participants are grouped according to the grade level(s) in which they are interested. Instructors are members of the AIMS Instructional Leadership Network. Supplies for the activities and a generous supply of take-home materials are included in the enrollment fee. Sites are selected on the basis of applications submitted by educational organizations. If chosen to host a workshop, the host agency agrees to provide specified facilities and cooperate in the promotion of the workshop. The AIMS Education Foundation supplies workshop materials as well as the travel, housing, and meals for instructors.

AIMS One-Week Perspectives Workshops

Each summer, Fresno Pacific University offers AIMS one-week workshops on its campus in Fresno, California. AIMS Program Directors and highly qualified members of the AIMS National Leadership Network serve as instructors.

The Science Festival and the Festival of Mathematics

Each summer, Fresno Pacific University offers a Science Festival and a Festival of Mathematics. These festivals have gained national recognition as inspiring and challenging experiences, giving unique opportunities to experience hands-on mathematics and science in topical and grade-level groups. Guest faculty includes some of the nation's most highly regarded mathematics and science educators. Supplies and take-home materials are included in the enrollment fee.

The AIMS Instructional Leadership Program

This is an AIMS staff-development program seeking to prepare facilitators for leadership roles in science/math education in their home districts or regions. Upon successful completion of the program, trained facilitators become members of the AIMS Instructional Leadership Network, qualified to conduct AIMS workshops, teach AIMS in-service courses for college credit, and serve as AIMS consultants. Intensive training is provided in mathematics, science, process and thinking skills, workshop management, and other relevant topics.

College Credit and Grants

Those who participate in workshops may often qualify for college credit. If the workshop takes place on the campus of Fresno Pacific University, that institution may grant appropriate credit. If the workshop takes place off-campus, arrangements can sometimes be made for credit to be granted by another college or university. In addition, the applicant's home school district is often willing to grant in-service or professional development credit. Many educators who participate in AIMS workshops are recipients of various types of educational grants, either local or national. Nationally known foundations and funding agencies have long recognized the value of AIMS mathematics and science workshops to educators. The AIMS Education Foundation encourages educators interested in attending or hosting workshops to explore the possibilities suggested above. Although the Foundation strongly supports such interest, it reminds applicants that they have the primary responsibility for fulfilling *current* requirements.

For current information regarding the programs described above, please complete the following:

Information Request

Please send current information on the items checked:

___ *Basic Information Packet* on AIMS materials	___ *AIMS One-Week Perspectives* workshops
___ *Festival of Mathematics*	___ *A Week with AIMS* workshops
___ *Science Festival*	___ Hosting information for *A Day with AIMS* workshops
___ *AIMS Instructional Leadership Program*	___ Hosting information for *A Week with AIMS* workshops

Name _____ Phone _____

Address _____

       Street   City   State   Zip